Words printed in **bold** are explained
in the glossary.

Acknowledgments
The publishers would like to thank Wendy Body for acting as
reading level consultant and Mark Daly for advising on
scientific content.

Photographic credits
Pages 7, 13, Tim Clark; page 31, Hutchinson Library.

Ladybird books are widely available, but in case of
difficulty may be ordered by post or telephone from:

Ladybird Books – Cash Sales Department
Littlegate Road Paignton Devon TQ3 3BE
Telephone 0803 554761

A catalogue record for this book is available
from the British Library

Published by Ladybird Books Ltd Loughborough Leicestershire UK
Ladybird Books Inc Auburn Maine 04210 USA

Your Body

written by CAROLINE ARNOLD
illustrated by LYNN BREEZE
and DEE McLEAN

Ladybird

Your amazing body

Can you imagine a machine that moves, eats, breathes, grows and can even repair itself when something goes wrong? Such an amazing machine does exist. That amazing machine is the human body!

Like other machines, the body has many working parts. Each part has a special job to do.

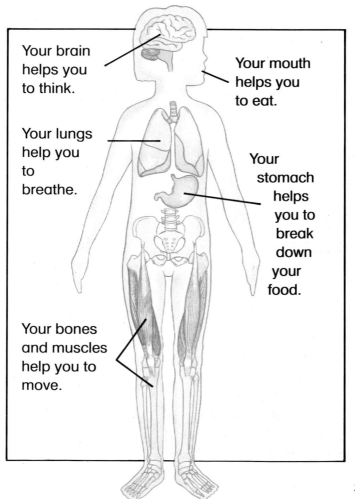

Your brain helps you to think.

Your mouth helps you to eat.

Your lungs help you to breathe.

Your stomach helps you to break down your food.

Your bones and muscles help you to move.

Your bones

Your bones are something like the poles inside a tent. They hold your body up and give it support.

The thick bones of the skull protect your brain.

The ribs protect your heart and lungs.

The bones in your back help you to stand up straight.

The long bones in your arms and legs help you to move.

You cannot see your bones. But you can feel some of them underneath your skin.

Although bones are very strong, they sometimes break when you fall. Doctors take X-ray photographs to see if a bone is broken.

This X-ray shows that two bones in the leg have been broken.

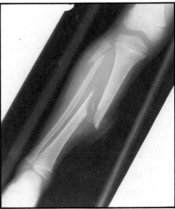

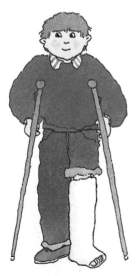

Broken bones are set in plaster so that they can mend in the right shape.

Your muscles

You use muscles every time you run, read, write, talk or eat.

Muscles are joined to bones. When muscles get shorter they pull your bones to make them move.

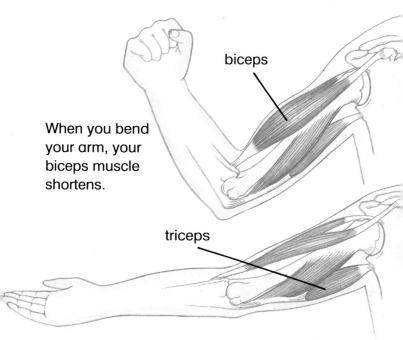

biceps

When you bend your arm, your biceps muscle shortens.

triceps

When you straighten your arm, your triceps muscle shortens.

There are over 600 muscles in your body.

Your heart and blood

Your heart is a special kind of muscle. It is about the size of your fist. It beats about seventy times a minute for the whole of your life.

You can hear a friend's heartbeat by listening through a paper tube placed on their chest.

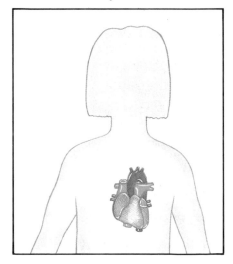

The *lub-dupp, lub-dupp,* is the sound of the heart valves closing as the heart beats.

The heart pumps blood through tubes or blood vessels called **arteries** and **veins**. They are like a network of tiny tunnels inside the body. Blood brings **oxygen** to all the parts of your body. Blood also takes away waste products that your body doesn't need.

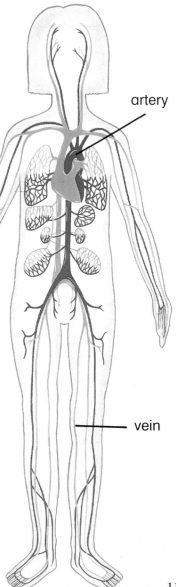

artery

vein

Your skin

Your whole body is covered by a tough outer layer – your skin. Your skin protects your body and keeps it clean.

Your skin contains a coloured substance or **pigment**. The pigment protects your skin from damage by sunlight. People with fair skins do not have much pigment in their skin. In strong sunlight they must be careful not to get **sunburn**.

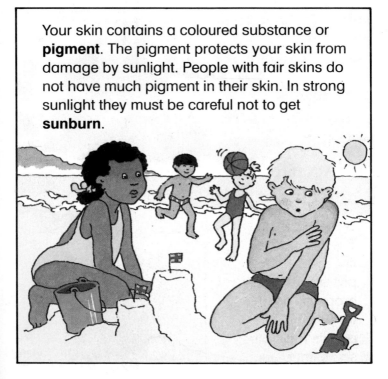

Your skin also keeps you warm or cool.

A layer of fat under the skin helps to keep you warm.

When it is hot, sweat comes out of your skin. As the sweat dries, it cools you down.

The skin on the fingertips has a pattern of ridges and grooves called a **fingerprint**. No two people have the same fingerprint.

Your fingernails, toenails and hair

Fingernails and toenails are part of your skin. They help to make the ends of your fingers and toes strong.

Hair is part of your skin, too. It protects your head and keeps it warm.

Some people have straight hair. Others have curly hair. What kind of hair do you have?

Hair, fingernails and toenails can't feel pain. That's why it doesn't hurt when you trim your nails or get a haircut.

Most people have about 100,000 hairs on their head. The hairs grow about 10cm each year.

Some people lose their hair when they get older. No one really knows why this happens.

15

Feeding your body

Everyone needs to eat and drink. Food and water contain all the things your body needs.

Like a car, your body burns fuel to get the energy it needs to move. Cars get energy from petrol or diesel fuel. Your body gets energy from foods that contain sugar, starch or fat.

Bread, butter, oil, beans and honey contain lots of energy.

HONEY

Foods that contain protein help
you to grow.

Meat, eggs, cheese
and milk contain
lots of protein.

Vitamins and minerals help to
keep your body healthy.

Vitamins help to build strong teeth and
bones and prevent certain diseases.
Iron is a mineral that is found in
green vegetables and meat.
Your body needs iron to
make blood.

What happens when you eat

Most of the food you eat is in large pieces. These pieces are too big to go into the blood. The digestive system breaks the food into smaller pieces so that it can be used by the body. It usually takes about six hours to digest a meal.

(1) When you chew, food mixes with **saliva** in your mouth. At the same time your teeth break the food into chunks.

(2) When you swallow, food travels to your stomach through a tube called the **oesophagus**.

(3) Your stomach is a large bag surrounded by muscles. It churns the food into smaller pieces and mixes it with more liquids.

(4) Food moves from the stomach into the small intestine and then into the large intestine. Because the food is now in tiny pieces, it can pass through the walls of the intestines into the blood stream.

(5) You get rid of the food that you cannot digest when you go to the toilet.

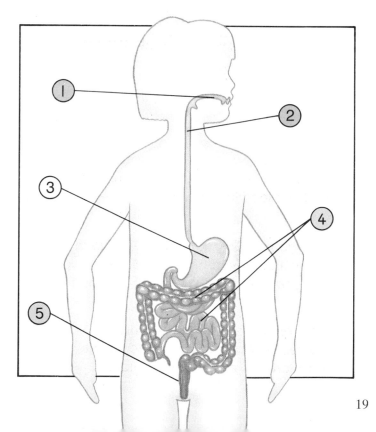

Breathing

Just like every other animal, you need oxygen to live. Oxygen is a gas in the air you breathe.

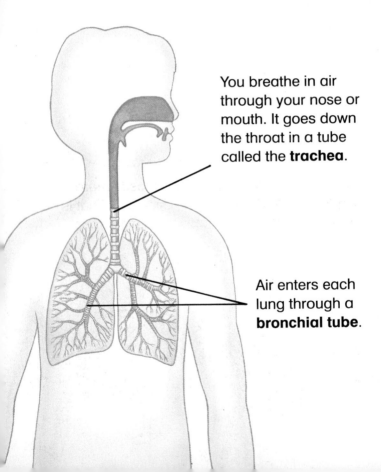

You breathe in air through your nose or mouth. It goes down the throat in a tube called the **trachea**.

Air enters each lung through a **bronchial tube**.

Each lung is like a balloon with many tiny pockets surrounded by small blood vessels. The blood in these vessels takes oxygen from the air and carries it to all the **cells** of the body.

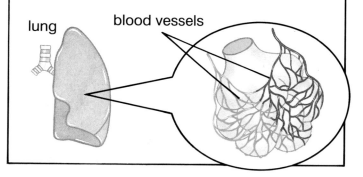

lung   blood vessels

When you exercise, your body needs more oxygen than when you are sitting still. That is why you breathe very heavily during a race.

Your senses

You have five senses that help you to know what is happening in the world around you. These senses are sight, hearing, smell, taste and touch.

Tasting

You use your tongue to taste the food you eat. There are small taste buds in your tongue that tell you if something is sweet, sour, salty or bitter. There are about 10,000 taste buds in your mouth!

Your taste buds for sweet things are at the tip of your tongue. Just behind them are the taste buds for salt. The back of the tongue tastes bitter things and the sides of the tongue taste sour things.

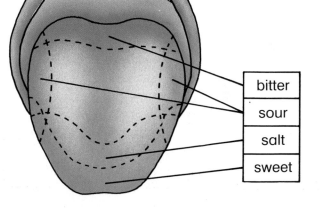

| bitter |
| sour |
| salt |
| sweet |

Seeing

Your eyes tell you about shapes and colours and how near or far things are.

Many people have eyes that do not work perfectly. The things they see look blurred. Glasses or contact lenses can help them to see more clearly.

Each eye is like a tiny, round camera.

The black part in the centre of your eye is called the pupil. It is a hole that lets light into the eye so that you can see a picture.

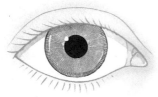

In the dark the pupil gets bigger to let in more light.

Any grit or dirt that gets into your eyes is washed away by tears.

You blink about 26,000 times each day.

Hearing

Your ears help you to identify sounds and to work out where they are coming from.

Listen to the noises around you.

Are they loud or soft?

Where do they come from?

What is making them?

You cannot see the part of your ear where you hear. It is inside your head. The outside of your ear helps to direct sounds to your inner ear.

Make a cone of paper and hold it up to your ear. It will catch more sounds and make them seem louder.

Many deaf people can work out what you are saying by looking at how your lips move when you speak. This is called lip-reading.

Smelling

You use your nose to smell things.

Some things smell nice. Others smell bad.

The things we like to eat usually have good smells.

Inside each nostril there are millions of tiny cells. As you breathe, these cells pick up smells in the air.

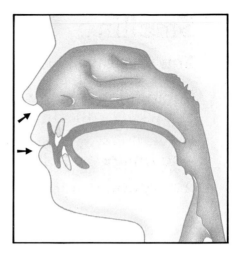

When you sneeze, air from your lungs rushes out through your nose at over 150 km per hour.

When you have a cold you cannot smell very well because the scents cannot reach the inside of your nose.

Touching

Your sense of touch is in your skin. Thousands of tiny cells help you to feel when something hurts. They also tell you if something is hot, cold, rough or smooth.

When you stub your toe you feel pain.

Heat from a fire feels good on a cold day.

A rabbit's fur feels soft and silky but tree bark feels hard and bumpy.

People who are blind can use their sense of touch to read braille. The letters are made up of patterns of little dots that stick up above the surface of the paper.

Your brain

The brain is a large, grey **organ** inside your skull. It is made of millions of tiny brain cells. You use your brain to learn and remember things and to work out problems.

The brain is connected to the rest of the body by nerves. The nerves are like a series of tiny electric wires. They carry messages to and from the brain.

It is your brain that tells all the parts of your body what to do and how to move.

Your brain works so fast you don't even notice it!

When you play catch, your brain sends hundreds of messages to your body. It says: *watch the ball, move your feet, raise your arms, catch the ball, close your fingers*. At the same time it receives messages about how the ball is moving and what your body is doing.

Growing up

Your body will change a great deal as you grow.

Life begins when a **sperm** cell from a man joins with an **egg** cell from a woman. For nine months this tiny cell divides and grows many times inside the mother. It becomes a baby.

Before it is born, a baby gets all the food and oxygen it needs from its mother.

A new baby is small and helpless.

Slowly it grows and learns how to do things for itself.

Boys and girls grow at about the same rate until they are around twelve years old.

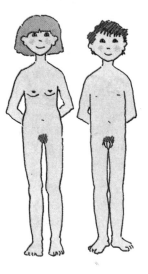

Just before the teenage years, the bodies of boys and girls begin to change.

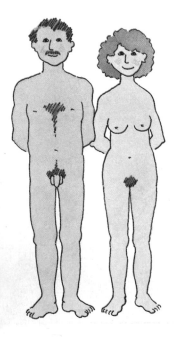

Over the next few years their bodies become like those of men and women.

Most people stop growing by the time they are about twenty years old.

Everyone is different

No two people are exactly alike.

Some are tall and some are short.

Some are fat and some are thin.

Even twins are different from each other in small ways.

People are many different sizes and shapes. They can also have different colour hair, eyes and skin.

Inside our bodies there are thousands of *very* tiny structures called **genes**. Genes control how you grow and the way you look.

You get your genes from your parents. That is why many children look like their parents.

Apart from identical twins, no two people have exactly the same set of genes. That is why there are no two people in the world who look exactly alike.

Repairing your body

What happens when you scratch or cut yourself?

Does it hurt?

Is there blood where the skin has been broken?

One of the most amazing things about your body is that it can heal itself when it gets sick or hurt.

New skin grows over a cut or scratch. A scab protects the skin underneath while it is healing.

When you are ill you may have a fever, feel achy, or have an upset stomach. It usually takes a few days for your body to get rid of the germs that are making it sick.

A visit to the doctor

When you go to the doctor for a check-up, the doctor makes sure that each part of your body is working the way it should.

Your height and weight show how much you have grown.

A thermometer measures your body temperature.

A stethoscope helps the doctor to listen to your heart and lungs.

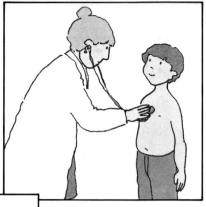

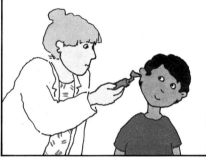

The doctor looks at your ears and throat with a bright light.

An eye chart helps the doctor to measure how well you can see.

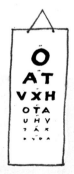

A strong healthy body

Keep your body healthy.

- Eat good food every day
- Do plenty of exercise
- Get enough rest

With good care, your body is a machine that will last a long time.

Food provides everything you need for energy and growth.

Exercise helps to make your muscles strong.

Sleep helps your body to get ready for a new day.

Glossary

artery A blood vessel that carries blood away from the heart.

bronchial tube A tube that carries air from the trachea to the left or right lung.

cell The very small units that make up the body.

egg The cell a woman makes in her body that can be fertilised and grow into a baby.

fingerprint The pattern of ridges on the skin at the fingertips.

genes Very small structures inside cells that control what a person looks like.

oesophagus The tube in the neck that carries food from the mouth to the stomach.

organ A part of the body that does one particular job.

oxygen A gas in the air that all animals need to stay alive.

pigment A coloured substance.

saliva The spit in the mouth that mixes with food.

sperm A cell a man makes in his body that can fertilise an egg.

sunburn Red, sore skin that has been damaged by too much sun.

trachea The tube leading from the mouth to the bronchial tubes.

vein A blood vessel that carries blood to the heart.